P9-DHH-442

SHARKS

GREAT WHITE SHARKS

JOHN F. PREVOST

ABDO & Daughters

Published by Abdo & Daughters, 4940 Viking Drive, Suite 622, Edina, Minnesota 55435.

Library bound edition distributed by Rockbottom Books, Pentagon Tower, P.O. Box 36036, Minneapolis, Minnesota 55435.

Printed in the United States.

Cover Photo credit: Peter Arnold, Inc.

Interior Photo credits: Peter Arnold, Inc.

Edited by Bob Italia

Library of Congress Cataloging-in-Publication Data

Prevost, John F.
    Great white sharks/ John F. Prevost.
        p.   cm. — (Sharks)
Includes bibliographical references (p.23) and Index.
    ISBN 1-56239-469-X
1. White shark—Juvenile literature. [1. White shark. 2. Sharks.] I. Title. II. Series: Prevost, John F. Sharks.
QL638.95.L3P73 1995
597'.31—dc20
                                                    95-1511
                                                        CIP
                                                        AC

ABOUT THE AUTHOR

John Prevost is a marine biologist and diver who has been active in conservation and education issues for the past 18 years. Currently he is living inland and remains actively involved in freshwater and marine husbandry, conservation and education projects.

Contents

GREAT WHITE SHARKS AND FAMILY

Sharks are fish without **scales**. A rough covering of tiny **denticles** protects their skin. Sharks do not have bones. Their skeleton is made of a tough, stretchy tissue called **cartilage**.

The great white is a large, active shark. Because of its powerful jaws and teeth, the great white is known as a superpredator. A **predator** is an animal that hunts and eats other animals as food. A superpredator is a predator that can hunt and eat other predators. Other sharks related to the great white are the mako shark, salmon shark, and porbeagle shark.

The great white shark is large and active.

WHAT THEY LOOK LIKE

The great white shark is shaped like a large torpedo. Adult females are larger than adult males. Females may reach at least 26 feet (8 meters) in length. Males may reach 18 feet (5.5 meters). Great white sharks that weighed over 2,500 pounds (1,134 kilograms) have been caught on rod and reel. Larger ones have been tangled in nets.

Named for its large white underbelly, the great white shark is mostly a dull blue gray.

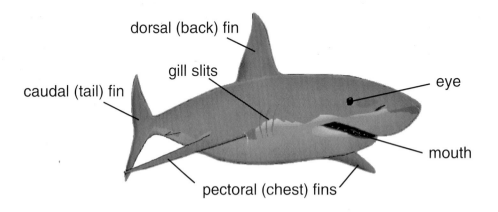

dorsal (back) fin

gill slits

caudal (tail) fin

eye

mouth

pectoral (chest) fins

The great white shark is shaped like a large torpedo.

Compared to other shark **species**, the great white is rarely seen or caught. It usually travels alone or in pairs.

WHERE THEY LIVE

Great white sharks are found in **tropical** and **temperate** oceans around the world. They will swim along coastlines or far offshore. They can be found near the surface—even in surf. Or they can swim in deep water. One great white was hooked at 4,200 feet (1,280 meters) deep.

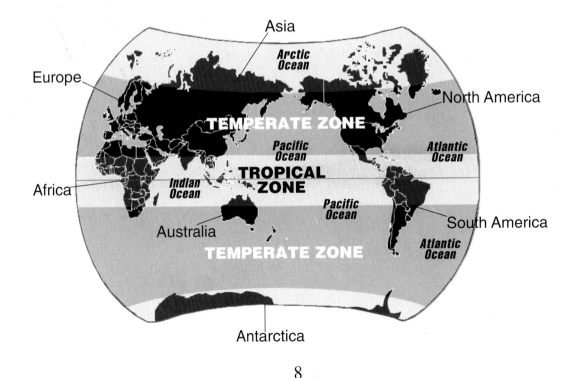

8

Great white sharks will swim near the water surface.

Great white sharks are a rare **species**. The smaller great whites live in **temperate waters**. Larger ones travel where they find food.

FOOD

All sharks eat other animals. The great white shark is the most powerful **predator** of all the fish. It can eat anything swimming in the ocean, including crabs, **shellfish**, **squid**, other sharks, and bony fish.

The larger great white sharks can catch and eat porpoises, dolphins, seals, **sea lions**, and sea otters. They will even feed on garbage thrown from ships or shore. Great whites also eat birds and whales.

The great white shark is the most powerful predator of all fish.

SENSES

For a fish to grow as large as a great white shark, it must find plenty of food and avoid enemies. A great white's eyesight is fair but only in clear, well-lit water. The other senses (taste, smell, and touch) are fully developed and work well in all kinds of water.

Sharks can sense **electric fields**. All animals give off a weak electric field. The skill to sense this field allows the great white shark to find hidden **prey**.

Although the shark cannot see the animal,

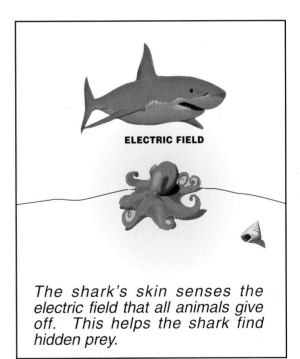

ELECTRIC FIELD

The shark's skin senses the electric field that all animals give off. This helps the shark find hidden prey.

A great white shark's eyesight is fair—but only in clear, well-lit water.

the shark's skin senses the **electric field** coming from the animal's body. This sense tells the shark that **prey** is nearby.

BABIES

A baby shark is called a pup. It is not known where female great white sharks give birth. But smaller great white sharks are found in **temperate** waters. This might be where young great whites are born. The pup is born alive after it hatches from its egg inside the mother.

Pregnant great white sharks are very rare. They may not give birth often. And since they are so large—possibly larger than 26 feet (8 meters)—they are hard to catch!

Experts believe great white sharks have their pups in temperate waters. This is a great white near the Barrier Reef in Australia.

ATTACK AND DEFENSE

The great white shark has large, triangle-shaped teeth in 5 to 6 rows, with 22 to 26 teeth per row. Each tooth has a saw-like edge to make cutting easier. A large adult over 20 feet (6 meters) long has nothing to fear except man, a larger great white shark, or hunger.

A smaller great white relies on its speed and good senses to avoid **predators**. The great white shark does not look for trouble. It will turn and swim away if it senses danger.

The great white shark has large, triangle-shaped teeth.

ATTACKS ON HUMANS

Because of its size and the number of reported attacks, the great white shark is one of the most dangerous sharks to man. But there are only 3 to 4 great white shark-attack deaths reported yearly all over the world. Fishermen kill millions of sharks each year.

The great white shark is a dangerous fish. But since it is rare, few swimmers will ever see one.

Because of its size, the great white shark is
one of the most dangerous sharks.

GREAT WHITE SHARK FACTS

Scientific Name: *Carcharodon carcharias*

Maximum Size: 18 feet (5.5 meters) males
26 feet (8 meters) females

Where They're Found: All over the world in **tropical** and **temperate** oceans.

The great white shark.

GLOSSARY

Cartilage (KAR-till-ij): A tough and stretchy type of tissue, like gristle.

Denticle (DEN-tih-kull): A small tooth-like structure that protects the skin of a shark and will make it rough to the touch.

Electric field: The electric-charged area surrounding an animal's body, created by the nervous system.

Gill slits: A part of the body of a fish by which it gets oxygen from water.

Pelvic fin: A fin found at the lower part of a fish's body.

Predator (PRED-a-tor): An animal that hunts and eats other animals.

Pregnant: Having one or more offspring in the females womb.

Prey (PRAY): An animal that is hunted for food.

Scales: Platelike structures forming all or part of the outer covering of certain animals, such as snakes and fish.

Sea lion: Any large seal found mainly in the Pacific Ocean.

Shellfish: Any animal having a shell and living in water, like a shrimp or lobster.

Species (SPEE-seas): A group of related living things that shares basic characteristics.

Squid: Sea animals related to the octopus that are streamlined in shape and have at least 10 arms.

Temperate (TEM-prit): Moderate to cool water located between the polar and tropical waters.

Tropical (TRAH-pih-kull): The part of the Earth near the equator where the oceans are very warm.

BIBLIOGRAPHY

Paul. *The Life of Sharks*. London: Weidenfeld and Nicolson,

о, Leonard. *FAO Species Catalogue Vol. 4, Sharks of the* nited Nations Development Programme, Rome, 1984.

. W., ed. *Sharks, Skates, and Rays*. Maryland: Johns Press, 1967.

Index